COLOUR

This book is t
the last da

PROOF

Girls from Guadeloupe in red, green and yellow; girls from Guadeloupe dressed in the colours of their country's flag.

A colourful collection of carnival colours – these French children join in the parade.

Long lines of British soldiers dressed in red and black;
long lines of British soldiers all dressed to look alike.

Lots of soldiers wear red all around the world.
Look, these Kenyan warriors are all in red as well!

Look at the colourful saris all in a row. In the temple the Indian women put on a really bright show.

Who are these men all dressed in orange robes? They are Buddhist monks from Thailand – off to the temple they go.

Great rivers of red dye pouring down from above –
it's a ceremony in India and it looks like good fun!

There's a party in Bali and to help the celebrations, people have made a statue from rice paste. It's decorated with lots of bright colours – doesn't it look great?

In Japan a woman wears white make-up – it's an old-fashioned way of making herself beautiful.

It's not just ladies who wear make-up either. This man in **Papua New Guinea** paints his face for a fête.

In Mali these houses are colourful and fun. This house has been painted with pictures of animals.

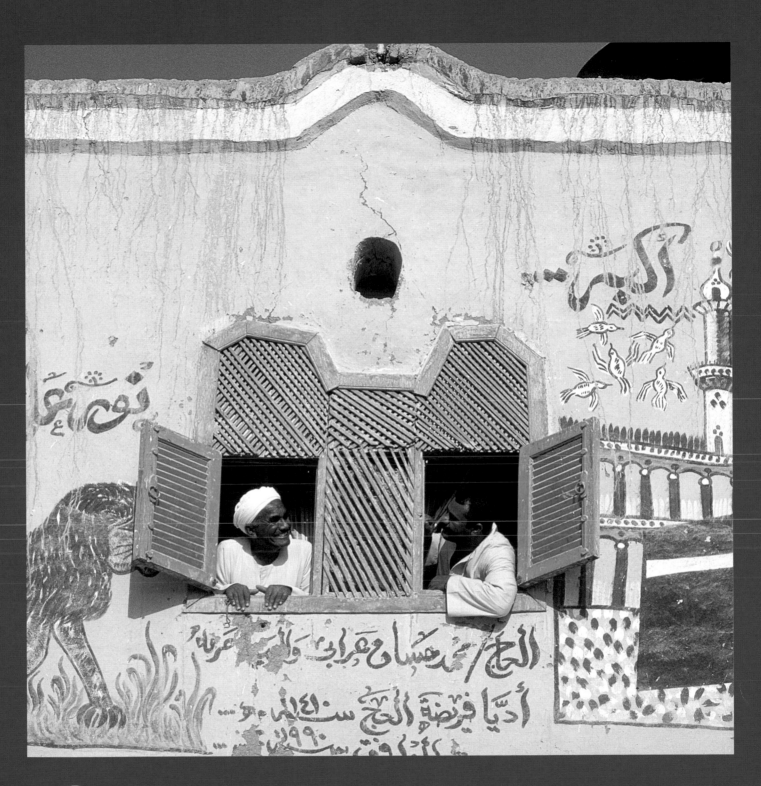

In Egypt, too, a house has been painted. The people who live there are pleased with the pictures!

This house in Argentina is a real work of art, with beautiful bold colours painted all over the walls.

In Morocco the robes the women wear have been painted on the sides of this house.

Even at night there are colours to be found. In America the cities glow bright with shining lights.

In Mexico, too, the lights burn bright, but here it's the buildings that glow in the night.

Bright, bold patterns on the rugs the woman sells, they are just like the patterns this Peruvian woman wears.

In a market in Madagascar there are rolls of shiny, bright cloth draped like colourful waterfalls.

Long bands of coloured cloth lie stretched out in the sun.
This Indian woman has dyed them and waits for them to dry.

What a colourful place this Moroccan spice market is with red sweet pepper, the yellow saffron and orange harissa.

This farmer from the Netherlands is growing tulips to sell. Broad strips of yellow flowers cover the fields.

Strips here too, but they're purple this time. These workers in France are collecting lavender.

Millions of little berries in a great big tub – this American man is making juice from these red berries.

What is the bright green plant growing in this field in Vietnam? It's rice and it likes wet places like this!

Like a shower of orange raindrops, rice pours out through the air. In Vietnam this is how they dry out all the rice.

In Malaysia they pick tea, the leaves of this plant. It grows in great, green fields that cover the land.

Like a rainbow in baskets, these Indian pigments for dye
are lined up in a shop for the people to buy.
How many different colours can you spot?